Reading & Writing Activities
for Character Education

Grades 3–5, Reading Level 3.5–5.0

Author: Jessica Franzene
Illustrator: Tom McKee

EP035 © 2010 Lab Safety Supply Inc.• 401 S. Wright Road • Janesville, WI 53547
www.edupressinc.com
ISBN 13: 978-1-56472-238-6

Table of Contents

Teacher's Guide for Appreciation (pages 4 and 5)

Jason comes to realize how much his parents do for him and is encouraged to both appreciate their thoughtfulness and to reciprocate by doing things for them.

Concepts to Consider

The story reflects a common trap for children and adults alike. The habit of taking for granted what others do for us is an easy one to fall into. We only realize the other party's contributions when they stop providing what we've come to expect. Jason learns to feel genuine appreciation for the work his parents do, but he also gets a taste of how good it feels when someone else appreciates his contributions. This give-and-take aspect of appreciation is healthier than just gratitude; it teaches the child how good it feels to have one's efforts appreciated, and conversely, how bad it feels to be taken for granted.

Discussion Questions

- How often do you think Jason said "thank you" to his parents before this day?
- How did Jason's parents feel about doing things for him? How did they feel about Jason's lack of appreciation for them?
- What are some things that people do for you that you don't usually say "thank you" for? How much time do these people spend taking care of you?

Teacher's Guide for Caring (pages 6 and 7)

Alexis cares so much for her cat that she lets it outdoors when she isn't supposed to and becomes responsible for the death of a mother bird. She makes a decision to care for the bird's eggs.

Concepts to Consider

Alexis clearly cares about her cat, which she can't stand to see cooped up inside. However, she has to face the consequences of her tenderheartedness—she knows that there is a risk to a mother bird. One thoughtless moment and Alexis is responsible for three unhatched eggs. She and her friend decide to commit themselves to caring for the baby birds, which will be a difficult project. Alexis must also decide if she is angry at her cat for killing the bird and deal with her parents' reaction to her disobedience. Her actions were a result of caring about the cat, but she has hopefully learned that sometimes caring also means acting responsibly.

Discussion Questions

- What does Alexis show she cares about in the story? How does she show she cares about these things?
- Do you think Alexis acted wrongly in letting her cat out? Why do you think so?
- Tell about a time when you cared about an animal or a person. What did you do that showed caring?

Appreciation

"Mom!" Jason hollered. "Where's my uniform?"

"By your book bag," she called back. She sounded exasperated, but Jason didn't notice.

He raced downstairs. If he didn't hustle, he'd be late for practice. His dad was already out in the garage, waiting for him. As he changed, he remembered it was his turn to bring bottled water for the team.

"Mom!" he bellowed again. This time, he heard his mother stalk to the bottom of the stairs. She was in the middle of an important project for work, and Jason knew he shouldn't interrupt her, but he had to bring that water!

"If this is about the water," she said wearily, "your dad already packed it in the car. We remembered, even if you didn't."

Jason raced to the door, but his mother stopped him.

"You know," she said, "your dad and I do a lot for you, and it would be nice if you showed us some appreciation now and then."

Jason shrugged and slipped out from his mother's grasp.

Practice went by quickly, and when Jason got home, he was starving. Usually, his mom or dad had a snack waiting for him, but today the dining room table was empty.

"Hey," he said to his dad, "where's my snack?"

His dad shrugged. Jason hesitated a moment, then went to the refrigerator and got some sandwich supplies out.

"Hey, make me one, too," his dad suddenly said.

"Me, too," his mom called from her office.

Jason frowned. He was incredibly hungry, and now he had to make three sandwiches before he could eat! He slapped the meat, mayonnaise, and bread together, and left his parents' sandwiches on the counter.

Just as he was about to take a huge bite, his mom yelled,

"Where's my sandwich?"

"Yeah, mine, too," his dad said.

"Oh, come on," Jason protested. "I worked so hard at practice, and there was no snack when I got home! The least you can do is let me eat."

His mom came into the living room, and both she and his dad chuckled.

"This isn't about the least we can do," his dad pointed out. "It's about the least you can do."

Jason reluctantly brought his parents their sandwiches. "What do you mean, the least I can do?" he asked, as he finally sat down to eat.

His mother said, "When you put on a clean uniform, or sit down to a meal, or get rides to practice, your father and I deserve a 'thank you.' You need to understand how hard we work to make your life happy, safe, and fun."

Jason chewed and thought. He realized that when he got home from practice, he'd usually eat the snack that was waiting for him, change into clean clothes, throw his dirty uniform on the floor, and go outside to play. Today, he decided, he would change that pattern.

"This is a good sandwich," his dad said, interrupting Jason's thoughts. "I appreciate you making it for me."

"Thanks," Jason said. It felt good to hear that. Then he said, "Thanks for driving me to practice. And Mom, thanks for washing my uniform."

"You're welcome," both of them said at the same time. Jason laughed. They'd both said it with their mouths full of sandwich.

Appreciation

Writing Activities

1. Write about what will happen next week on soccer practice day.

2. Make a list of things that Jason could do to help his parents. Make a list of words that he could use to tell them he appreciates all they do for him.

3. Write about a time you did something for someone else. How did he or she show appreciation? How did it make you feel?

4. Write about how it feels to do something for someone else when the person doesn't show appreciation.

Reading Comprehension Questions

1 Jason's mother sounds "exasperated." What do you think this means?

a) tired
b) irritated
c) happy
d) lost

2 Do you think Jason will throw his dirty uniform on the floor today? Why or why not?

_____

_____

_____

_____

3 Jason's parents are lazy. Is this a fact or an opinion?

a) fact
b) opinion

4 What is the main idea of the story?

a) Jason leans how to make sandwiches for the family.
b) Jason's parents get mad at him.
c) Jason learns to appreciate what his parents do for him.
d) Jason learns to pick up his dirty clothes.

5 What do you think Jason's parents talked about while he was at practice?

_____

_____

_____

_____

Caring

"Don't look at me like that," Alexis said to her cat, Trixie. "You know you aren't allowed to go outside. Mom said not to let you out."

Trixie meowed miserably and looked out the window, then glanced back at Alexis.

"I can't let you out," Alexis said sadly. She felt so sorry for Trixie, who loved going outside and chasing squirrels and birds. However, Mom was right—there was a robin with a new nest just outside the front door. If Trixie caught the bird, then the eggs in the nest would fail to hatch.

Alexis wished that the robin had built its nest in someone else's yard—someone who didn't have a cat.

Trixie meowed again, and Alexis couldn't take it anymore.

"I suppose if I watch you, then you can't get at the robin," she said. She opened the door, and Trixie ran outside. Alexis followed.

As she sat on the front stoop, keeping an eye on Trixie, Alexis heard someone call her name.

"Hey, Alexis, want to play Frisbee?"

Alexis leapt off the stoop and raced across the yard to David's house, catching the Frisbee as he tossed it from his front porch steps.

After a half hour, Alexis suddenly gasped—she'd forgotten about Trixie! "I have to get back," she said to David. She explained about the robin, and David followed her back to her yard.

"Trixie!" Alexis called. The cat was nowhere to be found.

David, who was walking to the tree to check on the nest, said, "Uh-oh." Alexis heard him gulp.

"What is it?" Alexis said. Her heart was beating fast.

"It looks like Trixie got to the robin," David said. "There are some feathers over here."

Alexis's eyes filled with tears, which she blinked away. She looked up at the nest. Dad had climbed the tree and had seen three tiny blue eggs in it.

"What's going to happen to the eggs?" David wondered.

"We have to save them," Alexis declared. "It's my fault that the mother bird died. I have to do something to help."

She climbed the tree and carefully brought the nest down. They took it into the garage, and David helped her look up information on the Internet.

"Okay, now we know we have to keep the eggs warm," Alexis said. "I'll ask my mom and dad to help me set something up."

It's going take a lot of effort to feed them," David said. He was reading a wildlife rescue page. "They need to eat almost all the time."

Alexis printed off the page and read the directions. "I don't care if I have to get up every hour of every night," she said. "I'm going to take care of them."

"I'll help," David said. "I can take them home on some nights. Hey, by the way, are you mad at Trixie?"

Alexis thought about David's question. Hatching the robin's eggs was going to take a lot of time and effort—and she was going to lose a lot of sleep. She was quite certain that her mom and dad were going to be annoyed with her for letting the cat out when she wasn't supposed to.

"Well," she finally replied, "I'm not angry at Trixie, because she was just acting naturally. It was my own fault for letting her out. It's just that I felt so sorry for her! She loves to be outside. I guess I'm mad at myself."

David nodded. "You didn't do it to be cruel to the robin or the eggs," he pointed out. "You did it because you care about Trixie."

"That's true," Alexis agreed. "But I care about the robin and her eggs, too."

Caring

Writing Activities

1. Write about what will happen when the eggs hatch.

2. Make a list of ways that Alexis could have taken her cat outside without danger to the robin.

3. Write a poem about a cat and a bird who are not enemies.

4. Pretend you are David. Write a journal entry about what happened on this day.

Reading Comprehension Questions

1 **What kind of bird did the cat kill?**

a) bluejay

b) crow

c) robin

d) woodpecker

2 **Put the events in order:**

a) looked up information on Internet

b) played Frisbee

c) let Trixie out

d) got the nest out of the tree

3 **What do you think will happen the next time a bird builds a nest in Alexis's yard?**

_____

_____

_____

_____

4 **What is another word for "miserable"?**

a) unhappy

b) terrified

c) crazy

d) stuffy

5 **Does David live close to Alexis? How do you know?**

_____

_____

_____

_____

_____

Teacher's Guide for Citizenship (pages 9 and 10)

Devon's complete disinterest in the presidential election is turned around by the realization that some citizens had to fight for the right to vote. He witnesses his mother mark her ballot and connects the act with the subsequent election results.

Concepts to Consider

The election story focuses on an act of citizenship—voting. Some view voting as a right and others as a duty. It is helpful to put it in perspective for children by pointing out that in the not-too-distant past, some citizens were barred from participating in the act. Devon's parents argue over whom to vote for, implying that their votes will cancel each other's out, yet they still make the effort. Note that Devon realizes that voting is "a big deal" when he finally juxtaposes the act with not being allowed to vote. An important part of being a good citizen is to understand how a nation's past informs its present.

Discussion Questions

- Do you think that Devon's parents vote because they want to, or because they feel they should? Why do you think so?
- Is it important to the story that Devon's parents are voting for different people? Why do you think so?
- Do you think people should vote? Why do you think so?

Teacher's Guide for Cooperation (pages 11 and 12)

In the aftermath of Hurricane Katrina, rescue workers, shelter volunteers, and caring individuals worked together, yet individually, to care for the pets that survived the storm.

Concepts to Consider

Cooperation can take many forms. Children are probably most familiar with a cooperation scenario where individuals work directly together to accomplish a job. In the "relay race" form of cooperation, each individual accomplishes smaller feats that add up to one big achievement. The example of the efforts to save pets after Hurricane Katrina illustrates this concept clearly for children. Although the individuals seem to be far removed from the end result, the truth is that without the efforts of each person, the goal may not be reached.

Discussion Questions

- Do you think the workers who rescued the animals from the homes ever met the people who adopted the pets? Why or why not?
- Do you think some workers were more important than others in the story? Why or why not?
- What do you think would have happened if people did not cooperate after the hurricane?

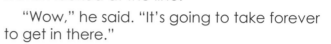

"That's not true!"

"Sure, it is!"

Devon groaned. "Not again," he said. His parents had been arguing for weeks, and with the presidential election just days away, it was worse than ever.

Devon wondered if his parents would ever agree about who should be president. He also wondered if he would ever care about who was president. The election was on Tuesday, and he couldn't wait for it to be over.

He couldn't even escape the subject in school. Ms. Carlson had been teaching about voting, elections, and democracy for weeks. It was so boring!

His mom and dad tried to get him interested in voting.

"When you turn 18, you can vote in all the elections," his dad pointed out.

"Big deal," Devon grumbled.

"Listen," his mother said. "Not so long ago, there were lots of people who couldn't vote. They weren't allowed. People had to fight to get the laws changed so that everyone had a chance to help choose the president. Voting is an important part of being a citizen."

Devon tried not to yawn.

His father laughed. "I'll tell you what," he said. "When your mother and I go to vote on Tuesday, we will take you with us. You can see for yourself."

That night, Devon tried to study, but he kept thinking about what his mother had said. Was it true that some people hadn't been able to vote in the past? Devon couldn't imagine what that would be like. He didn't think voting was a big deal, but not being allowed to vote sure seemed like one.

On Tuesday, Devon's parents picked him up after school. They were having another debate about the presidency.

"How do you know who to vote for?" he asked.

"Well," his mother said, "you learn about our country's past and present and decide what you'd like the future to be. Then you choose the person whose opinions are most like yours."

They had reached the voting place by then. As they walked to the building, Devon looked at the line.

"Wow," he said. "It's going to take forever to get in there."

"It'll move quickly," his mother said. "Besides, having to stand in line to vote is a small price to pay."

Devon remembered what she had said about people not being able to vote. They had spent a lot of time to get the laws changed, so standing in a long line didn't seem so bad.

Once they were inside, Devon watched the voters go into the booths. People went inside, pulled the curtain shut, and voted in private. Devon watched their faces when they came out. Some looked happy and some serious.

"Look at all the workers," he said to his dad. Many people were busily helping voters. Some of the helpers looked exhausted.

"They've been here since early morning, and they'll be here late tonight," his dad said.

As they approached the voting booth, Devon hung back.

"Come on in with me," his mother said. "You can watch me mark my ballot."

She pulled the curtain shut, and Devon watched as she voted. Seeing the candidates' names on the ballot was cool. He'd seen these people on television and read about them in the news, and now his mom was deciding between them. Devon had to admit it: he felt like he had witnessed a part of history. Tonight when he watched the news and saw the vote totals, he would know his parents' votes made a difference.

Citizenship

Writing Activities

1. Write about what might happen while Devon and his parents watch the news tonight.

2. Write about a time when you voted on something. Did your choice win?

3. Pretend you are Devon, and you are writing a letter describing election day.

4. Write about how it would feel if everyone else got to vote on something, but you weren't allowed. How would it feel not to have a choice or have your opinion listened to?

Reading Comprehension Questions

1. Do you think Devon will be interested in the results of the election? Why or why not?

_____

_____

_____

_____

2. What does "approach" mean?

   a) hang back

   b) move toward

   c) run fast

   d) hide from

3. Put the events in order:

   a) close the voting booth curtain

   b) stand in line

   c) mark the ballot

   d) watch the election results on television

4. How do the voting helpers look? What is another word for "exhausted"?

   a) grumpy

   b) bored

   c) energetic

   d) tired

5. What does Devon's mother tell him that changes Devon's mind about voting?

   a) that his father likes the wrong candidate

   b) that he should listen to his teacher

   c) that some people hadn't been allowed to vote

   d) that helpers worked long hours

Cooperation

Have you ever worked on a school project with a group of classmates? Have you ever played tug-of-war? If you have, you know that sometimes it's easier to get things done if you are in a group—especially if everyone works together.

We call working together "cooperation." But did you know that you can also cooperate with someone by dividing up a big job? Picture a relay race. In this kind of race, each member of the team runs a part of the distance. Then another runner takes over. When the competition is over, each runner has only run part of the race, but the runners have all accomplished the goal.

This form of cooperation was important after Hurricane Katrina hit the Southern coast of the United States in September 2005. Katrina was a destructive storm that caused huge floods. More than 2,000 people died. Hundreds of thousands of people lost their homes. Rescue workers did everything they could to help.

But people were not the only ones left without homes. Countless animals had no shelter, food, or water. When the storm hit, thousands of people had to leave their flooded homes. They were not allowed to bring their pets to the shelters with them. About 80,000 animals were stranded. Many people did not know they would not be able to go back to their homes for weeks, or even months. They didn't even know if their homes were still standing. They had no idea what had become of their dogs, cats, and other pets.

People from across the country came to the animals' aid. These people worked separately. But, as in a relay race, each shared the same goal: to help the animals.

The first part of the job was to reach the animals. Rescue workers took boats across the dirty floodwaters. They entered empty homes to look for pets. They climbed onto rooftops where dogs and cats waited for their owners to return. Sometimes the animals were too afraid to come near the workers. When that happened, the workers would leave food and water for the pets. Then they would try again the next day. They would not give up.

Once the animals were rescued, the rescue workers took them to an emergency shelter. This was a special place outside the city for pets that had just been rescued. There, other workers first checked the pets. If they were injured, they took care of their wounds. If they were sick, they gave them medicine. Of course, the pets needed fresh water and food. Other workers made sure that they had plenty of both.

When the animals were healthy enough, they had to be moved. But they could still not go back to their homes. The pets needed safe places to live until their owners could take them home. Sometimes, the owners could not be found, and new homes had to be found for the pets.

People all over the country offered their help. Animals traveled as far away as Wisconsin, California, and Maine to find new homes. Many people took care of animals in their homes until they were ready to go back to their owners. They fed them and gave them the affection and attention they needed. Sometimes people agreed to take in an orphaned cat or dog temporarily until a home could be found. But many of those people fell in love with the animals and adopted them permanently.

Cooperation

Name:_____

1. Write about a time when you cooperated with people in a group all at the same time.

2. Write about a time when you cooperated with people by doing an individual job that helped work toward a common goal.

3. Pretend you are a pet that was rescued after Hurricane Katrina. Write a thank-you letter to all the different people who helped.

4. Pretend you are a rescue worker. Write a journal entry about an animal you helped.

Reading Comprehension Questions

1 **What does the word "hurricane" mean?**

a) a volcanic explosion

b) a tropical storm

c) a sandstorm

d) a shooting geyser

2 **Put the events in order:**

a) Rescue workers find as many animals as they can.

b) Hurricane Katrina hits the U.S. coast.

c) People must leave their homes to escape the flood.

d) Shelters help reunite pets with their owners.

3 **Pets left behind were in danger. Is this a fact or an opinion?**

a) fact

b) opinion

4 **How do you think the workers felt about the animals? Why do you think so?**

_____

_____

_____

_____

_____

5 **True or false? Workers could not find new homes for abandoned pets.**

a) true

b) false

Teacher's Guide for Courage (pages 14 and 15)

Harriet Tubman finds the courage to escape from her captors and risks her life to help other slaves escape North. Along the way, she inspires other people to discover the depths of their own courage.

Concepts to Consider

There are many examples of courageous behavior in the passage. At the top of the list, of course, is Tubman's extraordinary achievement. To make a solitary break for freedom, with only a rudimentary knowledge of the outside world, took supreme effort and bravery. However, the fact that she went back—19 times!—elevates her to real-life superhero status. Is courage contagious? Surely Tubman's fearlessness gave others the confidence to make the escape. In turn, news of successful escapes led to other bids for freedom. The example of one's neighbor harboring escapees led to self-examination and then to participation in the Underground Railroad. Examples of courage such as Tubman's help us tap into the potential of our own resilience and fortitude.

Discussion Questions

- In what ways did Harriet Tubman show courage?
- Who else showed courage?
- Is there a time when you used your courage to help someone else? Tell about it.

Teacher's Guide for Fairness (pages 16 and 17)

The Jefferson siblings are frustrated with the age-appropriate rules their parents have instituted and struggle to understand why their older siblings are able to do things that they cannot.

Concepts to Consider

The aspect of fairness that is discussed in this story is perhaps the hardest for children to understand, because it seems arbitrary. While they may not understand why their parents set the age rules they did, the children are forced to realize that once the rules are in place, it would be unfair to change them. It seems unfair that the older siblings have privileges the younger ones don't, but each child is corrected in their inaccurate assumptions of unfairness.

Discussion Questions

- Was any child actually being treated unfairly?
- Tell about a time when you thought a family rule was unfair.
- Tell about a time when someone you know thought a rule was unfair, and you thought it was fair.

Courage

Imagine living in a world where someone else gets to tell you what to do, all day long, every single day. Do you feel like that sometimes describes your world, between schoolwork and chores at home?

There was a time in this country when the laws let people own other people, in order to make them do all the work. This system, called slavery, was a thousand times worse than just having to do homework and pick up your room.

Slaves had to work hard every day. They never were paid for their work, and they had to stay with the people who treated them so badly. They weren't allowed to decide where they worked, where they lived, or even where their children would live. They were trapped.

Harriet Tubman was born a slave. She lived in the American South and, like many African Americans, was forced to work hard from the time she was a little girl. In a way, being treated like this made her strong. It gave her the courage to escape from the world of slavery. Harriet made her way north all alone, sneaking through woods and swamps, hiding from slave catchers and their dogs. The journey must have been very frightening, but it was worth it. Once she made it to the North, she was free from the bonds of slavery.

You might think Harriet would have just stayed put to enjoy her freedom. After all, she deserved it after her courageous journey. Instead, Harriet snuck back into the South!

Why would she do such a dangerous thing? Harriet knew other people in the South wanted to be free. She wanted to help them because she knew not everyone had the courage to do it on his or her own. Harriet felt a need to show others that escaping to the North was possible. She knew that people could find the courage inside themselves if she showed them the way.

In all, Harriet made 19 trips back and forth to the South. It became more dangerous for her each time she went. Sometimes she had to wear a disguise. During this time, she guided more than 300 other escaping slaves over hundreds of miles to freedom.

The journey to the North was long and scary, but many "free" people helped along the way. These people were against slavery, so they started a secret route to freedom. It was called the Underground Railroad. Wouldn't it be frightening to hide escaping slaves, knowing that you and your family could get into big trouble? The people along the Underground Railroad risked everything to give food and shelter for people seeking freedom.

Later, the North and South went to war over slavery. Harriet again traveled south to help more people. She went with the Northern army to where the slaves were and got them away from the people who treated them badly. At one plantation, or farm, Harriet helped free 750 people!

Although she knew that what she was doing was right, some people believed Harriet was bad. These people supported the system of slavery and felt that Harriet was "stealing" when she helped slaves escape. They were very angry at her and at the other members of the Underground Railroad. But Harriet never stopped trying to help others, no matter how many people chased her or hated her. She knew that every person had the right to be free.

Courage

Writing Activities

1. Pretend you have escaped to freedom. Write about whether the frightening journey was worth it.

2. How would you convince a frightened person that escaping to freedom is possible?

3. Pretend you were guided to freedom by Harriet Tubman. Write her a letter telling her how you feel.

4. Make a list of the things you would need, and need to do, if you were hiding people in your house for the Underground Railroad.

Reading Comprehension Questions

1 **With whom did Harriet Tubman escape?**

a) her parents

b) by herself

c) other slaves from her plantation

d) the Northern army

2 **How many people did Harriet help on one plantation alone?**

a) 570

b) 75

c) 750

d) 80

3 **Did Harriet and other slaves escape to the South or to the North?**

a) South

b) North

4 **Why do you think that Harriet sometimes wore a disguise?**

_____

_____

_____

_____

_____

5 **What does "slavery" mean?**

a) working for other people

b) owning other people

c) renting land from people

d) escaping to freedom

Fairness

Mr. Jefferson looked at his three children. He tried not to laugh. Hannah, the oldest, was frowning. Jenna, the middle child, was frowning, and Tyler, the youngest, was scowling, too.

"What's the matter with you?" he asked. The kids all looked at him. Tyler spoke first.

"Mom won't let me walk to school by myself tomorrow! Hannah and Jenna get to walk alone whenever they want! It's not fair!" Tyler burst out.

"Actually, it is perfectly fair," Jenna pointed out. "Hannah and I couldn't walk to school alone until we were 10. You're only nine."

"That's true," Mr. Jefferson said. "Jenna, why are you so upset?"

"Mom won't let me stay out until 11 o'clock tomorrow night," Jenna complained. Her scowl returned. "It's not fair! I am not a baby anymore, so why can't I stay out later? Hannah gets to stay out late!"

"It's perfectly fair," Hannah corrected her little sister. "I couldn't stay out until 11 o'clock until I was 16. You're only 14."

"That's true," Mr. Jefferson said. "Hannah, what seems to be the problem with you? You look as frustrated as your brother and sister."

"It's not fair," Hannah responded instantly. "Mom won't let me borrow the car tomorrow night to drive all my friends to the movie theater."

"It's perfectly fair," Mr. Jefferson said. "You know the rule: you can't use the car after dark. In a couple of years, when you are 18, you can take the car at night."

He looked at the kids—none of them seemed any happier than when this conversation had begun. Mr. Jefferson sat down at the table across from the kids.

"Listen," he began. "I know it's hard for you to understand these rules. It's especially hard for the younger kids, because you see the older ones getting to do things that you're not allowed to do yet."

The younger kids nodded.

"I also under-stand that it's hard for Hannah. She's the oldest, but she still has to wait to be old enough to have permission to do a lot of things."

Hannah nodded.

"However," Mr. Jefferson continued, "your mother and I are not going to change the rules just because they make you unhappy."

"We understand that, Dad," Jenna said. "But we still don't think the rules are fair. Tyler wants to walk to school alone, I want to stay out late, and Hannah wants to drive the car at night. What's wrong with any of those things?"

Mr. Jefferson sighed. "There's nothing wrong with doing any of those things. You all just have to wait until you're old enough to do them."

All three kids spoke at once. "But that's not— "

"Fair," Mrs. Jefferson finished. She was listening at the door. "Maybe you don't think it's fair now," she pointed out, "but Jenna and Hannah, how would you feel if I told Tyler he could walk to school now, instead of waiting until he was 10? Hannah, how would you feel if we let Jenna stay out until 11 o'clock, even though she's not 16? The three of you need to believe that we are fair parents. We can't give each child different rules."

"Is that fair?" Mr. Jefferson asked the kids.

The kids thought it over.

Fairness

Writing Activities

1. Write an ending to the story.

2. Make a list of things you are old enough to do and another list of things you cannot do yet.

3. Write about a time when you thought a rule was unfair.

4. Pretend you are Tyler. You are 10 years old, and you get to walk to school alone. Write a journal entry about how it feels.

Reading Comprehension Questions

1. What does "frustrated" mean?

a) slightly nervous

b) upset and annoyed

c) tired and hungry

d) barely listening

2. Who is the oldest child?

a) Hannah

b) Tyler

c) Jenna

3. Which parent talks the most in the story?

a) the father

b) the mother

4. Do you think the kids are happier at the end of the story or the beginning, or do they still feel the same? Why do you think so?

_____

_____

_____

_____

5. The Jefferson family's rules are too strict. Is this fact or opinion?

a) fact

b) opinion

Teacher's Guide for Generosity (pages 19 and 20)

Josie is thrilled with the success of a fundraiser, but she resents that one person gives her only three dollars. She learns that generosity is relative to what one has to offer.

Concepts to Consider

Josie's initial enthusiasm about the fundraiser is based on how much money she is getting from individuals. She finds the old man's three-dollar offering to be almost insulting and is irritated that she had to wait for such a paltry amount. But then she is made to realize the money means a lot more to the old man than she would have suspected. She and Mikey immediately try to think of a way to assist the old man, who clearly could use a little generosity himself. Note that Mom is also motivated to help after this, even though she'd known about the man's plight before. Sometimes it's easy to ignore an everyday problem, yet be generous after a dramatic event, such as the tornado that figures into this story.

Discussion Questions

- Who shows generosity in this story? Explain.
- Should the old man have given more money? Why or why not?
- Have you ever done something generous? How did it make you feel?

Teacher's Guide for Good Judgment (pages 21 and 22)

The British intend to burn down the White House, and First Lady Dolley Madison must decide what treasures to save and how to get them to safety.

Concepts to Consider

The full-size portrait of George Washington is something most children have seen, thanks to the efforts of Dolley Madison. She knew it was irreplaceable to our country. The First Lady's courage and logical thinking under extreme pressure make her an excellent role model, especially because one can point to the tangible result of her judgment. Also note that she showed good judgment in knowing when she had to leave to keep herself safe.

Discussion Questions

- Why do you think Dolley thought it was so important to save the painting?
- If Dolley had been caught by the British, would trying to save the portrait have been worth it?
- What are some other ways Dolley showed good judgment on this day?

Generosity

Josie honestly didn't know if she was nervous or excited. She hopped off the front steps and back up again, waiting for Mikey to come down the street.

The whole school was participating in a fundraiser. They were trying to raise money for the people in Oak Grove who had lost their homes in a tornado. Many of the families were staying in a shelter while their homes were being rebuilt. People were working hard to collect money to help, and Josie and Mikey were among them.

Finally, Mikey rode his bike up to her house. Josie could tell he was excited.

"Ready to get out there and work?" he asked.

Josie jumped off the step a final time, and the two raced down the street.

Many of the neighbors were outside, working in their yards. The tornado hadn't hit here, but the winds had knocked down trees, and people were busily cleaning up. However, almost all of them stopped what they were doing to listen to Mikey and Josie. As soon as they heard the words, "money for the tornado victims," they went inside and brought out money.

Josie was thrilled as the money piled up. Most people gave at least 20 dollars. Some people wrote checks and some gave cash. One little boy even gave them a jar of dimes that he'd been saving for a year! Mikey and Josie took turns carrying it.

By lunchtime, they'd covered more than two miles, and both of them were starving.

"Let's just go to two more houses, and then we'll take a break for lunch," Mikey suggested. Josie agreed. The jar of dimes was getting heavier by the second.

No one was home at the next house. They crossed the street and tried the next one, which was a tiny cottage in need of painting. An old man was slowly raking up leaves and twigs.

"Hello," he said.

Josie explained what they were doing, and the old man stopped working to listen.

"Let me see what I can do," he said. He went inside. Josie and Mikey waited.

After a long time, the old man came out. He handed Mikey some crumpled bills and said, "There you are, young man." Then he went back to work.

"Thanks," Josie said. They walked away from the house and Mikey looked at the money.

"Three dollars?" he asked. "That's not very much. I bet that jar of dimes has way more than that, and that was from a little kid!"

They'd waited that long for just three dollars? Josie rolled her eyes.

Her mother had lunch waiting. The kids ate hungrily while her mom counted the money. She uncrumpled the three dollar bills and said, "Who gave you these?"

Josie explained about the old man.

Her mother asked, "Was it an old white house with a big tree in front?"

Josie nodded.

Mikey said, "I can't believe how cheap that old man is!"

Josie's mom shook her head. "He shouldn't have given any money away," she said. "He can't afford it. He's very poor, and three dollars could buy food for a day or two."

Josie looked up from her sandwich. Suddenly, those three dollars meant a lot more to her.

Mikey was looking at her from across the table.

"Maybe we should do something nice for him," he said. "We could help him rake his yard."

Josie's mom went to the refrigerator. "I'll pack some snacks, and you can share with him," she suggested.

Generosity

1. Write a list of ways you can be generous.

2. Write about what happens after Josie and Mikey go back to the old man's house.

3. Write a list of reasons people might be in need of money for food, clothes, or shelter.

4. Pretend you are making a shopping list for someone who has lost everything in a tornado. Write down everything you can think of that they would need to replace.

Reading Comprehension Questions

❶ Put the events in order:

a) Josie and Mikey eat lunch.

b) The old man gives them three dollars.

c) A tornado goes through Oak Grove.

d) Josie waits for Mikey.

❷ What is a tornado?

a) a tropical storm

b) a sand storm

c) a wind storm

d) a lightning storm

❸ Who made lunch for Josie and Mikey?

a) the old man in the cottage

b) Josie's mother

c) they made lunch

d) a diner

❹ What were the neighbors doing in their yards?

a) cleaning up

b) building a bonfire

c) collecting money

d) painting their houses

❺ What do you think will happen next in the story?

_____

_____

_____

_____

_____

Good Judgment

In the War of 1812, the United States fought the British. The British soldiers came to Washington, D.C., and began to burn the capital city. The president of the United States, James Madison, was not at the White House because he was helping the American army.

President Madison's wife, Dolley, was at the White House. The British soldiers were coming, and they wanted to burn the White House down. Dolley had to make some difficult decisions. Would she wait at the White House until her husband came back, or would she leave? Many of the White House workers had already left. They were afraid of the British. Finally, Dolley learned that President Madison would not be able to come back to the White House until it was too late.

She made her decision: she and the few servants who were left would leave the White House. It was no longer safe to remain there. However, before she left, Dolley wanted to save some of the precious things in the nation's capital.

Dolley didn't have a lot of time. She didn't have a lot of room either. There were some wagons waiting, but the White House contained many treasures. Dolley knew this very well, because she had spent many hours decorating and organizing the White House. She had taken very good care of the treasures left by the first three presidents.

As Dolley collected precious items to save from the British, she found important papers that belonged to her husband. She also gathered some silver items, because she knew how valuable they were.

She heard the British army was getting closer. If she wanted to escape, she had very little time. Dolley went to a special room. Hanging on the wall was a life-sized portrait of President George Washington. The painting was in a huge, heavy frame.

The frame was attached to the wall with screws.

This painting was one of the most important things in the White House. Dolley needed help saving this treasure. She called some servants into the room to help her.

At first, the servants and Dolley tried to unscrew the painting from the wall. As the British army got closer to the White House, Dolley knew that she was out of time. There was only one thing she could do. She told her helpers to break open the frame and pull the painting out. There was a chance that it would be damaged. Still, that was better than leaving it for the British to burn.

Finally, the men got the painting free from the frame and wall. Dolley made sure that it was placed on one of the wagons, and then she escaped from the White House.

Later, Dolley met up with President Madison. They saw the rest of the city burn. After the fire, they went back to the White House. Dolley was sad to see the building in ruins. She was relieved that she had managed to save some of its valuables, especially the painting.

Today, George Washington's portrait again hangs in the White House. Dolley Madison's good judgment is the reason this treasure still exists.

Good Judgment

Writing Activities

1. Write a different ending to the story.

2. Pretend you are Dolley Madison. Write a letter to a friend explaining why you saved the items that you did.

3. Write about a time when you showed good judgment.

4. Pretend you are President Madison. Write what you would say to Dolley after she told you the story of saving the painting.

Reading Comprehension Questions

1 **What does the word "portrait" mean?**

a) an important paper

b) a song about someone

c) a drawing or painting of someone

d) a poem about someone

2 **Was the painting Dolley's favorite thing in the White House? Why do you think so?**

_____

_____

_____

3 **The painting of George Washington was very beautiful. Is this fact or opinion?**

a) fact

b) opinion

4 **Was Dolley frightened of the British soldiers? Why do you think so?**

_____

_____

_____

_____

5 **Where does the painting hang today?**

a) a museum in Washington, D.C.

b) Dolley Madison's bedroom

c) the White House

d) the Pentagon

Teacher's Guide for Honesty (pages 24 and 25)

Sisters Maggie and Lacey forget to feed their dog in their excitement to go to a football game. They must decide whether to tell their father, knowing that he will be angry, and they will miss the game.

Concepts to Consider

Both Maggie and Lacey care about Major, and neither wants the dog to go hungry. However, Lacey is willing to be dishonest with her father in order to go to the game. Maggie doesn't want to miss the game or get in trouble either, but she is compelled to be honest with her father out of concern for the dog. Dishonesty would keep both girls out of trouble, but it would also cause the dog to suffer, and this is unacceptable to Maggie. The story ends before Maggie's confession, but it is clear that she and Lacey will both be in trouble.

Discussion Questions

- What do you think will happen next?
- How do you think Lacey will feel about what happens?
- Which sister is honest? Which sister is dishonest?

Teacher's Guide for Loyalty (pages 26 and 27)

Shawna has to consider the consequences to her friend, Emma, if she decides to leave her alone at recess to play with the more popular kids.

Concepts to Consider

Although Shawna sometimes gets impatient with Emma's quirks, she appreciates her friend's good qualities and is willing to disregard her imperfections. However, Shawna longs to spend time with the more popular kids and is tempted to do so when the opportunity arises. The story ends ambiguously. In a small but important passage, Emma shows loyalty to Shawna, letting her know she won't hold a grudge if Shawna chooses to leave her alone. Another layer of loyalty that can be explored is the relationship between Tory and her friends. This relationship is an example of misguided loyalty, born of insecurity. Shawna's loyalty toward Emma requires her to face her insecurities, while the more popular girls use loyalty to feel more secure.

Discussion Questions

- Who do you think Shawna runs after at the end of the story? Why do you think so?
- Do you think it would be fun to be friends with Emma? What about with Tory?
- If Shawna wants to make new friends, do you think that Tory and her friends are a good choice? Why or why not?
- How likely do you think it is that Emma and Shawna will remain friends and travel the world together?

Honesty

"It's your turn to feed the dog," Maggie said to Lacey.

"No, it isn't," Lacey insisted. "I fed him this morning."

"Well, I fed him twice yesterday, so you should feed him both times today," Maggie said.

The girls glared at each other. It was not that feeding Major was difficult; it was just that the girls were in a hurry. Their dad was going to take them to the high school football game tonight, and the girls wanted to get ready. They were going to paint their faces in the school colors and wear matching team sweatshirts.

"Let's get ready, and then we'll both feed the dog," Maggie finally suggested. The girls raced upstairs, changed into their sweatshirts, and then helped each other paint their faces with bright blue and white face paint.

"Are you two ready yet?" Dad called up the stairs. "It's 5 o'clock. We will have to hurry if we want to see the beginning of the game. It takes a half hour to get to the high school, and I'll have to search for a parking place."

"We're almost ready," the girls called. As they raced downstairs, Major barked at them.

On the way to the game, Maggie and Lacey sang the school song repeatedly, until Dad begged them to be quiet for just a minute. He stopped at the gas station and got out to fill up the car.

"Look at that funny dog," Lacey giggled. The dog was sitting in a parked car, looking out the window at them.

Maggie suddenly muttered, "Oh, no!"

"What's wrong?" Lacey asked.

"We forgot to feed Major," Maggie whispered.

Lacey groaned. Poor Major! He would get so hungry, waiting for the girls to come home. The game would last for hours. Dad usually took the girls out for ice cream afterward, so it would be midnight by the time they got home.

"What are we going to do?" Lacey asked her sister. "If we confess to Dad that we forgot to feed Major, he's going to be angry with us. Plus, he'll turn the car around and return home to feed him, and we'll miss the game."

"Yes, but if we don't tell him, poor Major will wait for us all night with an empty stomach. It's not good for him to go hungry like that," Maggie protested. She pictured Major sitting at home, whining. Maggie wanted to see the football game just as much as Lacey did, but it made her uncomfortable to think of the dog suffering.

Dad was nearly finished filling the car with gas. In a minute, he would go in to pay, and then they would be back on the road, heading toward the game.

"Just don't say anything," Lacey said. "Major will be okay for one night. We'll sneak food to him once we get home. We'll even give him extra. It'll be all right."

Maggie considered what Lacey had said as she watched Dad walk toward the car.

Maggie decided that Lacey was right about three things: Dad was about to be very mad, he would turn the car around, and they would miss the game.

Honesty

Writing Activities

1. Rewrite the story from the viewpoint of Major.

2. Write the conversation that Maggie has with her father.

3. Pretend you are Lacey. What might she write in her journal tonight?

4. Write about a time you were dishonest. How did it make you feel?

Reading Comprehension Questions

1 **Who is in charge of feeding the dog?**

   a) Maggie
   b) Maggie's father
   c) both Maggie and Lacey
   d) Lacey

2 **What do you think will happen if Maggie tells her father about forgetting to feed the dog?**

   _____

   _____

   _____

   _____

3 **What do you think will happen if Maggie does not tell her father?**

   _____

   _____

   _____

   _____

4 **What colors do the girls paint their faces?**

   a) black and white
   b) blue and green
   c) red and white
   d) blue and white

5 **What does "uncomfortable" mean?**

   a) feeling uneasy
   b) snuggly
   c) trapped
   d) honest

Loyalty

"Emma, pay attention!" Tory was practically shouting. Tory's friends all giggled.

Emma was at it again—she was gazing outside at a bird in the tree, instead of listening to the word she was supposed to spell. Tory had been furious when Ms. Martin put Emma on her spelling bee team.

Emma blushed, and Shawna did, too.

"Sorry," Emma stammered. "What was the word again?" Some kids laughed again and began to whisper.

Although Emma was Shawna's best friend, Shawna sometimes got impatient with her, just like everyone else did. Emma had trouble concentrating, and many of the kids made fun of her. Sometimes the teachers got upset with her. Shawna tried to help Emma as much as she could, but she couldn't help wishing that her friend would act a little more—well, normal.

At recess, Tory came up to Shawna and Emma. She was the most popular girl in fourth grade, and she decided who got to play kickball with the other popular kids.

"We need another player," Tory told the girls, tossing her hair. "I choose you." She pointed at Shawna.

For a second, Shawna was thrilled. She'd always wanted to play kickball with these kids! Then she looked at Emma. No one had to tell Emma that she wasn't wanted on the team. She knew. Tory and the other kids only paid attention to her when they were making fun of her.

Emma looked at the ground. If Shawna left her for the kickball field, Emma would spend recess alone. Usually, the two girls would sit under a tree and plan the adventures they would have when they were grown up. They would travel the world together. Emma loved talking about all the exciting places they would go. One day, they would be in France, looking at famous paintings in a big museum. The next day, they would travel to Egypt and visit the pyramids.

Today, the girls were going to plan their trip to the North Pole. Emma had looked it up on the Internet and was going to tell Shawna all about the journey.

"It's okay," Emma said softly. "Go ahead and play, Shawna. We can talk about the North Pole trip some other time." She smiled at her friend and started walking toward the tree.

Shawna looked at Tory, then at Emma's back as she walked away.

"What's the matter, Shawna?" asked Tory with an annoyed look on her face. "You'd rather hang out with *her*" she shot a dirty look at Emma "than with us?" Tory shook her head and started to walk off toward the kickball field.

Shawna stood in the same place for a moment. Then she called, "Wait!" and began to run.

Loyalty

Name:_____

1. Write two different endings for the story: in one, Shawna plays kickball with Tory, and in the other, she goes with Emma.

2. Write about a time when you made a new friend. Did it hurt your relationship with an old friend?

3. Rewrite the story from Tory's point of view or from Emma's.

4. Write about a time that someone was loyal to you. Did they stick to their plans with you even though someone else asked them to do something else? Did they speak up when someone was teasing you?

Reading Comprehension Questions

1 Why did Tory shout at Emma?

a) Emma couldn't hear her.

b) Emma was far away.

c) Emma was playing kickball without her.

d) Emma wasn't paying attention.

2 What trip were the girls going to plan at recess?

a) Egypt

b) Paris

c) the North Pole

d) Ireland

3 What does the word "furious" mean?

a) insulted

b) scared

c) angry

d) full

4 Put the events in order:

a) Emma tells Shawna to go ahead and play kickball.

b) Tory wants Shawna to play kickball.

c) Tory shouts at Emma to pay attention.

d) Shawna calls "Wait!" and starts to run.

5 Why did Shawna want to play kickball?

a) It's her favorite sport.

b) She was bored with Emma.

c) It was what all the popular kids were doing.

d) She didn't want to plan any more trips.

Teacher's Guide for Patience (pages 29 and 30)

Micah's patience is tested on a trip to the amusement park, both by his grandfather's slow pace and by the long lines for the rides.

Concepts to Consider

When greeted with the news that Granddad is coming along to the amusement park, Micah handles the situation with some grace. However, as the day progresses, he realizes he won't accomplish all he'd hoped for, and he loses his patience. The factors that try his patience are impersonal (long lines) and personal (his beloved Granddad). Both factors are rendered petty by Micah's realization that he is lucky that they are the only things slowing him down. Granddad is held back from doing much because of his age and condition. Once Micah gains perspective on this, we see him exhibit extreme patience by putting off riding the Twist and Turn in order to spend quality time with his Granddad.

Discussion Questions

- What happened that made Micah impatient? What happened that made Micah more patient?
- How do you think Grandad felt about going to the amusement park?
- Tell about a time when you lost your patience.

Teacher's Guide for Patriotism (pages 31 and 32)

Maddy relates her class's exploration of American history in her diary, detailing both the lessons she learns and her reactions to them.

Concepts to Consider

What, exactly, is "patriotism"? Is it reciting the Pledge of Allegiance without pausing to consider what the words mean? Is it hanging a flag, yet now knowing what its symbols stand for? Is it obeying the laws of the land without looking back at their legacy and evolution over the nation's history? Or is patriotism learning about the nation's history and being proud of the accomplishments of its citizens? It's important for children to learn about the history behind the symbols, the pledge, and the anthem's lyrics. A deeper body of knowledge about United States history can lead to a real love of country, rather than just going through the motions.

Discussion Questions

- What things have you learned about United States history that Maddy discusses?
- What are Maddy's feelings about the lessons she is learning?
- What do you think it would feel like to be president?

Patience

Micah couldn't stop smiling. His parents had finally agreed to take him to the amusement park! Roller coasters, chili dogs, and milkshakes were Micah's idea of a great time. He hoped there would be time to go on all the rides, especially the Twist and Turn. That night, he studied a map of the park to find shortcuts between the rides.

Micah knew there would be long lines, but he figured if he and his parents hurried, they could get to everything before the park closed. Maybe he'd hint to them that they should wear running shoes!

On Saturday morning, Micah was ready to go before his parents had even eaten their breakfast.

Finally, everyone was ready. They piled into the car. Micah sat in the back seat and counted his money while his dad drove.

When he looked up a while later, he saw his father was parking in front of the senior home where Micah's grandfather lived.

Dad must need to drop something off for Granddad, Micah thought. Oh, well. How long could that take?

Micah's parents both got out.

"Uh, what's going on?" Micah asked.

"We thought Granddad might enjoy coming along," his mother explained. She shut the car door.

Micah was alone in the car. He tried to imagine hurrying from ride to ride as Granddad tried to keep up. As much as Micah loved his grandfather, he knew that he was going to slow the day down.

After a moment, his parents came out with Granddad, who used a walker to get around.

"Hey, big guy," Granddad said as he climbed in the back seat. "Ready for some fun?"

Some fun is right, Micah thought.

The amusement park was very crowded, but after a few minutes of walking, Micah noticed that people were giving Granddad plenty of room to pass by with his walker. Sure, it took a little longer to get from place to place, but Granddad was having so much fun that Micah didn't mind very much.

"Look at that!" Granddad said, pointing to the Twist and Turn. Micah's heart sank when he saw how long the line was. It was already afternoon, and he'd only been on three rides!

"If I wait in line for that one, I won't have time to go on many more," he said. He was glad that Granddad was having fun, but if it wasn't for him, Micah would be far ahead in the line by now.

He was sick of being patient about the long lines and Granddad's slow walking. He kicked at the fence. Then he glanced over at Granddad. Granddad was watching the roller coaster with a sad look on his face.

"I bet that would be fun," Granddad said softly.

Micah swallowed. While he was making a big deal out of only having time to go on a few rides, Granddad was wishing that he could go on at least one.

They both were quiet for a moment as they watched the roller coaster.

"Hey, Granddad," Micah finally said. "I can go on this ride some other time. Let's spend the rest of our day just hanging out. Do you like chili dogs and chocolate milkshakes?"

Patience

1. Rewrite the story from Granddad's viewpoint.

2. Make a list of activities that Micah and Granddad could do together.

3. Pretend you are standing in a roller coaster line, and you begin talking to another kid in line. Write what you would say to each other.

4. Tell about a time when you were impatient with someone else. Did you wish you would have handled the situation differently?

Reading Comprehension Questions

1 **What does Micah's grandfather use to help him get around?**

a) a cane

b) Micah's parents

c) a wheelchair

d) a walker

2 **Will Micah take Granddad on a roller coaster? Why or why not?**

_____

_____

_____

_____

3 **Name three things that Micah is looking forward to doing at the amusement park.**

_____

_____

4 **What happens to make Micah decide not to ride the Twist and Turn?**

a) The line is too long.

b) The park shuts the ride down.

c) He feels bad that his grandfather can't go on the ride.

d) He gets sick.

5 **What is the main idea of the story?**

a) Micah realizes that, if he hurries, he can ride many rides.

b) Micah wishes his grandfather would hurry up.

c) Micah realizes spending time with his grandfather is more important than hurrying to get on as many rides as he can.

d) Micah learns to forgive his grandfather for moving so slow.

Patriotism

Dear Diary,

Our class is learning about the United States of America. I didn't know that the states used to be colonies! The people in the colonies had to listen to what the King of England told them to do. They were not free to make their own laws. I would not like to obey a king who lived across the ocean!

I'll write more tomorrow,

Maddy

Dear Diary,

The 13 red and white stripes on the flag stand for the colonies. The people in the 13 colonies wanted to become a country. They wrote to the King of England and told him they wanted freedom. It must have taken a lot of courage to do that! The king could have punished them—or even worse! I bet the king was furious when he read the letter, which was called the Declaration of Independence. Many people signed the letter, even though they knew they might get into trouble. Maybe that's why they call the United States the home of the brave!

More later,

Maddy

Dear Diary,

When we say the Pledge of Allegiance at school, we are promising to be loyal to the United States. "Pledge" means making a promise, and "allegiance" means to be loyal. We face the flag when we say the pledge because it helps us remember what it stands for. The 50 stars stand for the states, and I already told you what the stripes stand for. Tomorrow, I am going to ask the teacher what the flag's red, white, and blue colors stand for.

Maddy

Dear Diary,

Well, I asked the teacher about the colors of the flag. She said it was a very good question and helped me look up the answer. The red stands for courage and helps us remember the brave people who formed our country. The blue stands for justice. It helps us remember that all Americans are equal. The white represents innocence, which reminds us that the country needs to do good things. We also looked up pictures of older flags, from when there were fewer than 50 states. One flag had all the stars in a big circle!

Maddy

Dear Diary,

Today in class, we discussed the U.S. Constitution. The important laws of the United States are written in it. The Constitution protects our rights. There is a list of rights, which has been added to over the years. For instance, when the Constitution was first written, only white men who owned land could vote. That sounds pretty silly today, doesn't it? They changed that law, and now people of all colors, including women, can vote. It's good that people can change laws in this country. That means that we can change the stuff that isn't fair and become a better country. Too bad they don't let kids vote, though!

Maddy

Dear Diary,

Today we learned about George Washington, our first president. People admired and trusted him, because he fought so bravely during the war against England. It must have been exciting to be the very first president! Back then, the nation's capital was New York City—but now, it's Washington, D.C. Can you guess who the capital is named after? That's right: President George Washington!

Maddy

Patriotism

Writing Activities

1. Design a flag for a new country. Describe your design, including what the colors and symbols stand for.

2. Pretend you are Maddy. Write a new diary entry summing up all the things you have learned about United States history.

3. Write a poem about what it would feel like to live in a brand-new country.

4. Pretend you are George Washington and have just been elected president of a new nation. Write a journal entry describing how you feel.

Reading Comprehension Questions

1 **What did Maddy learn about on the first day?**

a) what the colors of the flag stood for

b) what the stripes on the flag stand for

c) about the original 13 colonies

d) about the Constitution

2 **What does the color red stand for in the flag?**

a) courage

b) justice

c) innocence

d) honor

3 **The flag's stripes stand for the 13 colonies. Is this fact or opinion?**

a) fact

b) opinion

4 **What is another word for "courage"?**

a) patriotism

b) citizenship

c) balance

d) bravery

5 **Does Maddy think these lessons are boring or interesting? Why do you think so?**

_____

_____

_____

_____

_____

_____

Teacher's Guide for Perseverance (pages 34 and 35)

Annie Sullivan is determined to make Helen Keller understand that people use words to communicate with each other. Both Annie and Helen persist in the face of their individual challenges and eventually succeed.

Concepts to Consider

The story of Annie and Helen features two individuals' struggles to achieve goals that others believe are unattainable. While Helen's plight is dramatic and captivating, students might have difficulty relating to it because of her unusual circumstances. Annie's perspective might be easier for students to grasp: she sees the big picture of Helen's struggle and is determined to find a way to break through to the girl. Helen's own brand of perseverance is nearly compulsive—while others have given up on her, she remains perpetually curious about the world around her. Annie's and Helen's struggles are related, but because of their individual circumstances and knowledge, they are dissimilar. Each, however, perseveres in the face of adversity.

Discussion Questions

- Why do you think Helen's family had given up trying to teach her?
- How do you think Helen felt when Annie first came to help her?
- Do you think Annie or Helen had to work harder? Why do you think so?
- Have you ever wanted to give up on a job because it was hard and you didn't know if you could succeed at it?
- What do you think would have happened to Helen if Annie had given up?

Teacher's Guide for Respect (pages 36 and 37)

Juan is excited that the one rule in his new class is to have respect for oneself and others. He quickly finds out that he has a lot to learn about the meaning of the word.

Concepts to Consider

The word "respect" is often used to remind children to defer to adults. However, the broader meanings of the word come into play in nearly every human interaction. Children can easily see that the little things we all do, including waiting our turn, keeping within our own personal spaces, not touching other people's property, etc., are all ways of showing respect. Mr. Hansen's clever rule, which also includes self-respect, can be used for just about any discipline issue that comes up in a classroom. Juan's initial enthusiasm for the one-rule classroom turns into dismay and then a grudging respect for the teacher's innovative take on classroom rules. His parents spur him to explore more into the meaning of the word "respect"—and Juan is a quick study.

Discussion Questions

- What do you think of the one-rule classroom idea?
- Tell about some other ways you can show respect for others.
- What are some ways that you can show self-respect?

Perseverance

Annie Sullivan was exhausted. Would she be able to sleep, or would she be awakened by another temper tantrum? Right now, Helen Keller was sleeping, but Annie knew that she might wake up at any moment.

Annie's mind drifted as she lay in bed. Was she doing the right thing? Everyone in Helen's family felt sorry for the young girl. They had given up trying to teach her and gave her everything she wanted, all because Helen couldn't hear or see. She had gotten very ill and gone blind and deaf when she was a baby, just as she was learning to communicate with other people. Because of this, Helen could not talk. She didn't know you could use language to show how you felt. She didn't know that people spoke words, wrote words, or used their hands to sign words.

Annie wanted to help Helen, but Helen didn't understand that. She seemed to think that Annie was her enemy. Annie was the only person who did not spoil Helen. Annie wanted to teach her how to communicate using language, not tantrums and tears.

As she lay awake that night, Annie decided to keep trying until she got through to Helen. She saw how smart the girl was and how she tried so hard to understand the world around her. Helen used her senses of touch, smell, and even taste. Helen might not know what words were, but she never stopped trying to make sense of what was happening, and to express her feelings about it.

Sometimes, when the girl lost her temper, Annie wanted to kick and yell along with Helen. It was so frustrating! Annie would hand Helen a doll. Helen would hold the doll in one hand while Annie signed the letters D-O-L-L into the girl's other hand. Would Helen ever be able to connect the spelled word with the object in her hand?

The night passed, along with many other nights. Annie worked with Helen for weeks. She tried many other ways to make Helen understand that objects, people, and even feelings have names. Some days, she wanted to give up, and she was sure Helen felt the same way.

Still, Annie and Helen kept trying. During one long and difficult day, Annie signed the word "water" into Helen's hand. Then she held her hand under the water pump so the little girl could feel it. Annie had done this hundreds of times before, and she thought she might have to do it a hundred more times.

As the water poured over her hand, Helen's face suddenly changed. Annie held her breath. Helen signed the word "water" into Annie's hand, and felt the water again. In that moment, Helen learned that everything had a name, and that people communicated through words.

When Annie went to bed that night, she was exhausted, as usual. But she knew that all her hard work had paid off. Helen understood! Annie's job now was to help Helen learn everything the girl wanted to know. She knew there was much hard work ahead of them both, but Annie was excited. Helen had never stopped trying, and Annie would not either.

Perseverance

Writing Activities

1. Helen Keller later learned to write and to read. What do you imagine her first diary entry might have said?

2. Pretend you are Annie. Write a journal entry for the day that Helen understood the word "water" for the first time.

3. Helen Keller lost her sight and her hearing when she was just a baby. Her sense of touch became very strong because she used it to explore her world. Make a list of words that describe objects in your classroom, using your sense of touch.

4. Write about a time when you had to do something that was hard. Did you want to quit? What made you keep going?

Reading Comprehension Questions

1 **What does "losing your temper" mean?**

   a) forgetting something

   b) looking for something

   c) getting angry

   d) going on a hunt

2 **Put the events in order:**

   a) Helen learns to communicate.

   b) Annie Sullivan comes to work with Helen.

   c) Helen goes blind and deaf.

   d) Annie helps Helen learn everything she can.

3 **What is one word that Annie spells into Helen's hand?**

_____

4 **How does Helen's family feel about her?**

   a) angry

   b) depressed

   c) frustrated

   d) lonely

5 **Does Annie quit working for Helen's family after Helen learns to communicate? How do you know?**

_____

_____

_____

_____

Respect

"There is only one rule in my class," Mr. Hansen said. "Respect others and yourself."

Only one rule! Juan couldn't believe his ears! This was going to be an awesome year. Every other teacher at Grove Middle School had a whole list of rules. Mr. Hansen was instantly Juan's favorite teacher. He couldn't wait to tell his parents about the one-rule classroom.

His mother grinned when Juan mentioned the rule at dinner.

"You think that's pretty cool, don't you?" she said to Juan.

"Of course I do," he said. "Mr. Hansen's crazy, though—with only one rule, he's going to have a lot of trouble keeping order in the classroom."

"What do you think it means to have respect for yourself and for others?" Juan's father asked.

Juan helped himself to more spaghetti while he thought about his father's question.

"Well," he said with his mouth full.

His mother held up her hand. "That's a good example," she said to him. "It's not respectful to other people to talk with your mouth full."

Juan chewed and swallowed, then said, "I guess it's not. I hadn't thought of it that way."

"What are some other things—" his father started to say, but Juan interrupted him.

"I bet we can get away with a lot in this class," Juan said.

"Is interrupting someone respectful?" his mother asked him.

Juan frowned. He supposed it wasn't. He reached across the table to take the last piece of garlic bread.

"Is it respectful to take the last piece without asking if anyone else wants it, or offering to share it?" his father asked. Juan sighed. He got the feeling that his parents were enjoying themselves. Maybe he'd been happy about the respect rule because he didn't really consider what the word meant.

That night, in his room, Juan looked up the word "respect" in his dictionary. There were several meanings, including treating others with good manners and with consideration.

He went downstairs to the living room, where his parents were reading. He started to tell them something, but thought better of it. He didn't want to hear them say, "Is it respectful to interrupt someone while they are reading?" He waited a moment, and then said, "Excuse me. Can I talk to you?"

"Of course," they said, and set down their books.

Juan explained what he'd read in the dictionary. "What does it mean to treat someone with 'consideration'?" he asked.

His mother explained, "It means that you think about what your words will mean to a person. You think about how you would feel if someone said them to you. It means that you show people they are important, that their feelings matter."

"You also show respect with your actions," his father added. "You respect other people's property and their space."

Juan sighed. He'd thought the one rule was cool, but it turned out that the word "respect" meant all the other rules rolled up into one big rule. No touching other people's stuff. No interrupting. No name calling. No talking back to the teacher. No distracting people from their work. No hitting. No teasing.

Still, Juan had to admit that Mr. Hansen was pretty smart. The respect rule was easier to remember than a whole list of rules. Maybe all the work in his class would be this easy!

Respect

Writing Activities

1. Pretend you are Juan. Make a list of actions that would break the "respect yourself and others" rule.

2. Pretend you are a teacher. Write a list of rules that would fit under the "respect yourself and others" rule.

3. Write about a time when someone was disrespectful of you. How did you feel?

4. Write about a time when you were disrespectful. What happened as a result?

Reading Comprehension Questions

1. What does "consideration" mean?

a) protecting others

b) cleaning up after others

c) thoughtfulness toward others

d) acting out

2 Name two things that Juan's parents said were disrespectful.

_____

_____

3. Name two ways that Juan learned about respect.

_____

_____

_____

4 It is likely that:

a) Juan will behave in class tomorrow.

b) Juan will not behave in class tomorrow.

c) Juan will tell Mr. Hansen he is wrong.

d) Mr. Hansen will not be Juan's favorite teacher anymore.

5 Do you think that Juan likes Mr. Hansen? Why or why not?

_____

_____

_____

_____

_____

Teacher's Guide for Responsibility (pages 39 and 40)

Charlie handles many adult responsibilities in order to help his mother make a better future possible for his family. He balances his desire for fun with his duties by combining the two.

Concepts to Consider

Although he is just a high-school student, Charlie has many adult duties. His mother relies on him to help with the day-to-day responsibilities, but he knows he also is contributing to the betterment of the family's future. Because his mother can rely on him, she is able to attend college. Charlie understands the big picture and resolves to be patient, hoping that his current burdens will someday be lifted if he stays on the right path. He addresses his concerns about losing his batting prowess by combining practice with duty as well as he is able. It is interesting to note that he intends to keep up his batting practice by helping his little brother learn the skill. Teaching his brother is another in a long line of responsible acts.

Discussion Questions

- How do you think Charlie's little brothers feel about him?
- How do you think Charlie feels about his little brothers?
- Tell about a time when you were responsible.

Teacher's Guide for Self-Discipline (pages 41 and 42)

Jack LaLanne makes a decision to live healthy, and he spends the rest of his life living up to his potential through hard work and self-discipline.

Concepts to Consider

While younger generations may associate Jack LaLanne with infomercials, the man's lifetime of incredible feats of strength is an excellent example of an average individual tapping into his or her potential. His initial decision to change his diet and exercise habits shaped his life. What is especially inspiring about his story is his influence on people, most of whom never even met him. By exercisng self-discipline, Jack LaLanne had a positive effect on not only his own life, but the lives of many others.

Discussion Questions

- How do you think Jack LaLanne felt when he thought back to the day he made his decision to change his habits?
- Have you ever made a simple decision that changed your life? Did it happen all at once or did the change take time and self-discipline?
- What are some times that you have not had self-discipline? What happened as a result?

Responsibility

The alarm clock rang. Charlie groaned. Could it really be 6:30 already? It seemed as though he had just fallen asleep.

He looked over at the clock hopefully. Maybe he had set the alarm for the wrong time. No, the numbers clearly said 6:30. Charlie groaned again.

From down the hall, he heard his baby brother crying. Charlie walked down to the baby's room and picked up the little guy. Mason, his five-year-old brother, came out into the hallway.

"Good morning," Charlie said to Mason. "Time to get ready for school."

Mason nodded and rubbed his eyes. "Is Mom already gone?" he asked Charlie.

"Yes," Charlie said. "She already left for school." He went downstairs to fix breakfast for his little brothers.

Things had been difficult since the boys' parents had gotten a divorce. Mom worked a lot, and when she wasn't at her job, she was at college. She didn't make much money right now, but if she finished school, she could earn a lot more. She left early in the day and sometimes got home late at night. The babysitter came to the house in the morning, but until then, Charlie took care of both of his brothers.

He helped Mason with his backpack. Mason was in kindergarten. His bus came a little earlier than Charlie's, so Charlie would walk him to the bus stop, wait with him, and then wait for his own bus.

By the time Charlie got to school, he already felt like he had put in a full day's work. His nights were filled with homework, chores, and helping with his brothers. He remembered what it was like before, when he could hang out with his friends after school, playing basketball and listening to music. Maybe after his mom finished school, things would go back to the way they had been.

"Hey, Charlie," Gavin Dawson called as he got on the bus.

Charlie sat down with Gavin.

"A bunch of us are going to try out for the baseball team," Gavin told him. "Do you want to? You're a good batter. We could use you on the team this year."

Charlie thought about how fun it would be to make the team.

"When does the team practice?" he asked Gavin.

"Every day after school for an hour," Gavin told him.

Maybe I could do it, Charlie thought. Maybe Mom could hire an after-school babysitter. If someone could watch Mason and the baby, then I could finally have some time for myself.

Then he remembered how much money it cost for a babysitter.

"I can't do it this year," he told Gavin. "Maybe next season."

"Well, keep practicing at home," Gavin said. "I'd hate to see you lose your batting talent."

Charlie thought about what Gavin had said. What if he forgot how to bat and then didn't make the team next year? How could he find time to practice when he had Mason and the baby to watch?

Finally, he thought of the solution. After school that day, he took his two little brothers into the backyard.

"Are you ready?" he asked Mason. He held out the small toy bat. Mason took it.

"Here," Charlie showed him. "You hold it like this."

Responsibility

Writing Activities

1. Pretend you are Charlie's mother. Write a note to him telling him how you feel about all the work he does.

2. Tell the story from Mason's point of view.

3. Make a list of chores you are responsible for doing.

4. Write about a time when you were irresponsible. Did your irresponsibility have an effect on other people?

Reading Comprehension Questions

1 **What do you think will happen next year during baseball tryouts?**

_____

_____

_____

2 **Do you think that Charlie likes baseball better than he likes his brothers? Why or why not?**

_____

_____

_____

3 **"Things had been difficult since the divorce." What is a synonym for "difficult"?**

a) loud

b) relaxing

c) hard

d) easy

4 **What happened that made Charlie decide to practice batting with Mason?**

a) Gavin told him to keep practicing so he could keep his batting skills.

b) Gavin told him he wasn't good enough to be on the team.

c) Mason wanted to try out for the baseball team.

d) Charlie was sick of sitting in the house all day.

5 **Put the events in the order they happened:**

a) gave Mason a plastic bat

b) rode the bus with Gavin

c) made breakfast for little brothers

d) showed Mason how to hold the bat

Self-Discipline

Jack LaLanne was 15 years old when he decided that he ate too much junk food. He decided to eat healthier foods and to exercise more.

That simple decision led to a lifetime of amazing accomplishments. Jack got so strong that he was able to swim for miles —while towing boats! He could do more than 1,000 push-ups in 23 minutes. He won many awards for his feats of strength. Even when he was nearly 100 years old, Jack still exercised for two hours every day.

Jack made a choice to eat right and to exercise when he was a teenager. Eighty years later, he was still amazingly healthy.

What happened in those 80 years, after Jack promised himself he would live healthily? Jack worked hard every single day. He made decisions to eat only healthy foods. He spent much of his time inventing new ways to exercise. He worked out by swimming and lifting weights every day. All these little choices added up to big results for Jack.

It must have been hard to resist junk food. Jack said that when he was a child, he loved sugary, fatty foods. Imagine what it was like the first few days after he decided to give them up. Each time he was hungry, he had to make the right choice. Each day, even if he was tired or didn't feel like it, Jack made the decision to exercise and lift weights.

Finally, all the hard work paid off. Jack was strong and fit. He wanted to show the world what he could do with his newfound strength. He began to perform amazing feats, such as swimming long distances in short amounts of time. He broke a world record for underwater swimming. He broke another for push-ups.

Naturally, people were amazed at Jack's strength. But Jack wasn't satisfied; he didn't want to show off. He wanted to inspire other people and help them get strong and healthy, too. He had designed several exercise machines, so he opened his own gym. He helped many men and women get fit and healthy. After several decades, there were hundreds of Jack LaLanne health clubs in the United States. By then, almost everyone had heard of him.

People couldn't wait to see his next show of strength. Jack was always thinking of new ways to test his body and inspire people. One time, he swam in the ocean while pulling a giant boat that weighed more than one ton. The swim was supposed to be one mile long. However, the waves kept pushing Jack backward. By the time he was finished, he had swum more than six miles.

On another swim, Jack towed 10 boats. The boats had 77 people total in them. Can you imagine what it would have felt like to be in a boat that was being towed by this man? Jack took them for a mile-long ride in less than one hour. The most amazing part of this accomplishment? Jack was 66 years old!

Jack LaLanne knew that people admired and looked up to him. It was important to him to set a good example and show people what they could do if they set their minds to it. He worked hard for many years to make his life better, and he helped many other people while he was at it.

Self-Discipline

Name:_____

Writing Activities

1. Pretend you went on a Jack LaLanne "boat ride." Write a diary entry about your experience.

2. Make a list of decisions you could make that would change your life for the better. Would these things take a lot of self-discipline?

3. Write about a time that you showed self-discipline.

4. Write about a time that someone inspired you to do something new that made your life better.

Reading Comprehension Questions

1 **What does the word "feat" mean?**

a) toes and ankles

b) disappointment

c) accomplishment

d) exercise

2 **How do you think Jack LaLanne felt about exercising? Why do you think so?**

_____

_____

_____

_____

_____

3 **Jack LaLanne wasted his time by exercising too much. Is that a fact or an opinion?**

a) fact

b) opinion

4 **How do you think that people felt when they saw Jack accomplish an amazing feat?**

a) impressed

b) depressed

c) confused

d) terrified

5 **Was Jack LaLanne a smart man? Why do you think so?**

_____

_____

_____

_____

Teacher's Guide for Tolerance (pages 44 and 45)

William Penn founds a new community, where people are allowed to live as they please—but they must treat others with the tolerance they expect for themselves.

Concepts to Consider

Having an attitude of true tolerance might best be described as "I respect you for your differences" rather than "I put up with your differences." William Penn's goal was to provide a place where people would not judge one another, but he also was mindful of human nature. He expected and planned for people's tendency to demand tolerance for themselves but to act intolerantly toward others. He was both practical and idealistic. His beliefs helped him to create a better life for many people.

Discussion Questions

- What things did William Penn think were unfair?
- How do you think the king felt about William Penn?
- Do you think it would have been scary to go to live in a new country across the ocean?
- Tell about a time when someone showed tolerance toward you.

Teacher's Guide for Trustworthiness (pages 46 and 47)

Amanda is enthusiastic about babysitting, but only because of the fun aspects. She fails to take the task seriously, and she discovers that she is unreliable and untrustworthy because of her decisions to skip babysitting classes and ignore a parent's instructions.

Concepts to Consider

Amanda is willing to take on the responsibility of babysitting, but only because she wants the money and the fun. Her willingness alone doesn't qualify her as a good sitter. But she is quick to realize this and to admit she needs help when her responsibilities prove too much for her. The story doesn't end with a resolution, only with her decision to seek help. Amanda might decide that babysitting is too much trouble, or she might resolve to live up to the trust that parents will put in her. Either way, she knows that she is currently untrustworthy and unreliable. That realization is a small first step in the direction of trustworthiness.

Discussion Questions

- What makes Amanda an untrustworthy babysitter?
- How do you think Benny felt when he saw that Amanda didn't know what to do about his ankle?
- What makes Amanda different from her sisters? How can Amanda change these differences?

Tolerance

Pennsylvania, one of the 50 United States, was named for the Penn family. Hundreds of years ago, William Penn decided to start a colony—a place where all sorts of people were welcome, and the rules were fair to everyone.

This was a new way of thinking for many people. Back in those days, people fought over which religion was right. They fought over whether women were equal to men. They fought over whether people of different races were equal.

William did not believe that religion, gender, or race mattered. He felt that all people were equal, and they should have the right to decide how to live. William's feelings were so strong that he broke the law by talking about how unfair things were in England. William was sent to jail for speaking about these issues. But it didn't stop him. He spoke out again and went back to jail. He did this six times!

Finally, William decided that the king of England would never let people have real freedom. He decided it was time to find a new place to live. He would go to the New World and create a new kind of society. He would let all people worship and live the way they wanted to.

William asked the king if he could take some of his followers, the Quakers, to the New World. The king agreed to let them go. William was glad, and no doubt so was the king. Now the king didn't have to put up with William making trouble all the time!

People followed William to Pennsylvania. They knew their lives would be better there. Women could get the same education as men. People could choose which churches to go to. Everyone would have to obey the laws, but the laws would be fair.

William was serious about making Pennsylvania a good place to live. But he couldn't do it all on his own. People who lived there had to leave each other alone. They couldn't pick on each other for being different.

If you came to live in Pennsylvania, you had to be fair. You didn't want to be bossed around, or picked on, so you had to promise not to treat others that way. You had to tolerate people's differences—and mind your own business!

People from around the world were impressed with Pennsylvania. It was hard to believe that you could go to a place and live in peace. People didn't hate each other for being different. Their lives were better because they could relax and not worry about being hated.

In addition to making sure the colonists treated each other fairly, William worked with the Native Americans. People who had started other colonies fought with the native people and chased them away. Many people believe that the Native Americans were too different to live near white people. William thought that was nonsense. He learned Native American languages so that he could talk to them. He bought land from them at a fair price. He wanted to live in peace with them.

William had succeeded. He'd created a new kind of place to live. His ideas and beliefs inspired many other people. He didn't just talk or write about tolerance. He acted on his beliefs, and he made the world a better place.

Tolerance

Name:_____

Writing Activities

1. Pretend you have moved to Pennsylvania from England. Write a letter convincing a friend to follow you.

2. Pretend you are William Penn. You have been sent to jail. Write a journal entry about how you feel.

3. Write a list of things that make you different from anyone else in the world.

4. Write a letter to the king explaining why you want to move to the New World and take your followers with you.

Reading Comprehension Questions

1 **How many times did William Penn go to jail?**

a) five

b) two

c) six

d) three

2 **What does the word "freedom" mean?**

a) following the king's laws

b) able to do what you want

c) telling other people what to do

d) having a schedule

3 **What were William Penn's followers called?**

a) Lutherans

b) Mormons

c) Shakers

d) Quakers

4 **Why did people follow William Penn to Pennsylvania?**

a) They wanted to be free to live their lives how they wanted.

b) The king didn't want them around anymore.

c) They were kicked out of England.

d) William Penn promised them riches in the New World.

5 **Do you think William Penn made the world a better place? Why or why not?**

_____

_____

_____

_____

_____

Trustworthiness

"Big bucks," Amanda announced to her reflection in the mirror. "Tonight is the night that I start earning big bucks."

For years, Amanda had watched her two older sisters go off to babysitting jobs. They would come back with lots of cash and funny stories about the little kids they watched.

Now, it was Amanda's turn. She figured that babysitting must be the easiest job in the world—you got to eat snacks and watch television, and you got paid for it.

Amanda's mom had signed her up for babysitting safety classes at the YMCA. What her mom did not know was that Amanda had stopped going to the classes after the first day. She knew how to take care of little kids. After all, she had heard her sisters' stories! How hard could it be? You played with them, read them stories, put them to bed, and then got the house to yourself.

Tonight, Amanda was going to take care of a four-year-old boy, Benny Miller. His bedtime was 8 o'clock, and Amanda was starting at 7 o'clock. She would only really be watching him for an hour. Then she would send him to bed, and watch television and talk on the phone until his parents came home.

Amanda walked to the Millers' house and rang the bell. As Mrs. Miller showed her around the house, Amanda's mind wandered. What would she do with all of the money she earned?

"And here's my cell phone number. Call me if anything happens," Mrs. Miller said. She left the note on the counter.

Mr. and Mrs. Miller left, and it was just Amanda and Benny. The little boy stared at her, and Amanda suddenly felt nervous. She wished she had paid more attention to what Mrs. Miller had been saying.

She also wished she had actually gone to the babysitting classes.

Time passed very slowly. Amanda tried reading to the little boy, but he did not pay attention. She tried playing cars with him, but he just cried for his mom and dad. Finally, it was 8 o'clock.

"Time for bed," Amanda said.

Benny ran down the hall away from her. After he turned the corner, she heard him scream, "Ouch! Ouch!" He began crying again, this time really loudly.

Amanda raced to him. Benny was on the floor, holding his ankle. Amanda pulled his hands away and saw that it was red and beginning to swell.

"Oh, no," she whispered. Suddenly, what had seemed like the easiest job in the world now seemed impossible. What should she do? She tried to remember stories her sisters had told. Should she try to find an ice pack? Should she wrap his foot up? Mrs. Miller had said something about a first-aid kit.

Amanda wished harder than ever that she had gone to the safety classes. How could she be trusted to take care of little kids? She could not even be trusted to pay attention to Mrs. Miller's instructions.

There was only one thing that Amanda could do. She went to the counter, picked up the phone, and dialed Mrs. Miller's number.

Trustworthiness

Writing Activities

1. Write an ending to the story. What do you think Mrs. Miller says to Amanda?

2. Make a list of things that Amanda can do to be a trustworthy babysitter.

3. Pretend you are Amanda. Write a note to Benny to tell him how you feel.

4. Pretend you are Amanda. Write a journal entry about your struggle to decide to tell your parents about skipping babysitting classes.

Reading Comprehension Questions

1 **Put the events in order:**

a) Benny hurts himself.

b) Amanda skips babysitting classes.

c) Amanda tries reading Benny a story.

d) Amanda calls Mrs. Miller.

2 **Do you think Amanda will babysit again? Why or why not?**

_____

_____

_____

_____

3 **Name two things Amanda thought would be fun about babysitting.**

_____

_____

4 **Benny gets hurt. How does this happen?**

a) He trips over a toy car.

b) He falls while he is running from Amanda.

c) He burns his hand on the stove.

d) He cuts his finger.

5 **What do you think Amanda will say to Mrs. Miller?**

_____

_____

_____

_____

Answer Key

Appreciation, page 5
1. b
2. Answers will vary.
3. b
4. c
5. How to teach him to appreciate what other people do for him. Answers will vary.

Caring, page 7
1. c
2. c, b, d, a
3. Alexis will keep the cat away from it. Answers will vary.
4. a
5. Yes. Answers will vary.

Citizenship, page 10
1. Answers will vary.
2. b
3. b, a, c, d
4. d
5. c

Cooperation, page 12
1. b
2. b, c, a, d
3. a
4. Answers will vary.
5. b

Courage, page 15
1. b
2. c
3. b
4. Answers will vary.
5. b

Fairness, page 17
1. b
2. a
3. a
4. Answers will vary.
5. b

Generosity, page 20
1. c, d, b, a
2. c
3. b
4. a
5. Answers will vary.

Good Judgment, page 22
1. c
2. Answers will vary.
3. b
4. Answers will vary.
5. c

Honesty, page 25
1. c
2. Answers will vary.
3. Answers will vary.
4. d
5. a

Loyalty, page 27
1. d
2. c
3. c
4. c, b, a, d
5. c

Patience, page 30
1. d
2. Answers will vary.
3. Answers will vary.
4. c
5. c

Patriotism, page 32
1. c
2. a
3. a
4. d
5. Answers will vary.

Perseverance, page 35
1. c
2. c, b, a, d
3. doll or water
4. c
5. No. Answers will vary.

Respect, page 37
1. c
2. Answers will vary.
3. Answers will vary.
4. a
5. Answers will vary.

Responsibility, page 40
1. Answers will vary.
2. Answers will vary.
3. c
4. a
5. c, b, a, d

Self-Discipline, page 42
1. c
2. Answers will vary.
3. b
4. a
5. Answers will vary.

Tolerance, page 45
1. c
2. b
3. d
4. a
5. Answers will vary.

Trustworthiness, page 47
1. b, c, a, d
2. Answers will vary.
3. Answers will vary.
4. b
5. Answers will vary.